TO RON
Helmut · DEZ. 04.

STATE STREET VILLAGE
ILLINOIS INSTITUTE OF TECHNOLOGY

HELMUT JAHN
Murphy/Jahn

LYNN BECKER
WERNER BLASER

FLASH
PRESS

State Street Village — Illinois Institute of Technology

First published in the United States in 2004 by Flash Press.
35 East Wacker Drive, Chicago, Illinois, 60601

Library of Congress Control Number: 2004116407

ISBN 0-9763994-0-7

Book layout by Werner Blaser, Keith Palmer and Tracy Erski.

Printed in Italy

CONTENTS

INTRODUCTIONS

State Street Village is an extraordinary addition to the IIT campus. Its innovative design elegantly addresses residents' needs, improves the university's appeal to prospective students, and transforms the appearance of State Street — the central artery of campus.

Completion of State Street Village, The McCormick Tribune Campus Center, and extensive landscaping marks the end of the first phase in the fulfillment of the IIT Master Plan.

The next phase is the renovation of key Mies Van der Rohe buildings including S.R.Crown Hall, a National Historic Landmark and Mies' signature effort. Spearheading the fundraising for Phase Two, the Mies Van der Rohe Society is integral in realizing the vision of the Master Plan. I am pleased Helmut Jahn is serving as a Mies Society board member.

LEW COLLENS
PRESIDENT, ILLINOIS INSTITUTE OF TECHNOLOGY

IIT's new dormitory, State Street Village, commences an initiative to redefine IIT as a residential university as well as continue the overall campus renewal begun by the adjacent McCormick Tribune Campus Center. This building faced a tricky task to provide the second new building to be built here in 30 years; SSV acknowledges the context of both enduring Mies van der Rohe (originator of the IIT's Main Campus and its architecture) and upstart Rem Koolhaas (architect of the first 21st century building here.) Murphy/Jahn had the grace to take suggestions from both, but end up with their own building: simple of intent, humble in materials, elegant in execution.

The dorm's design is achieved through a masterful command of project budget and schedule, and through Murphy/Jahn's intimate control of the construction process. It offers unadulterated materials and simple but elegant interiors. Murphy/Jahn-designed furniture populates throughout, durable and yet fitting to the building's refinement. Occupants have taken to the building's highly organized interiors, and dorm rooms bring in bright colors and multiple variations of furniture arrangement.

IIT now has another remarkable example of how to go "beyond Mies" and build for the 21st century. The SSV dorm is an artful, creative building solidly grounded in the concrete rationales of construction but going well beyond the conventional into innovative technologies, new materials, and environmentally conscious design. It holds up a taut, attenuated standard for ambitious architecture, responsive to local setting yet of a fresh and unexpected take on Modernism's idioms. The dorm defines the trajectory of Modernism for campus architecture, offering a compelling new contribution.

DONA V. ROBERTSON
DEAN, COLLEGE OF ARCHITECTURE
ILLINOIS INSTITUTE OF TECHNOLOGY

STUDENT HOUSING IN URBAN DESIGN

WERNER BLASER

The State Street Village student housing project is a new twist on dormitories for accomplished architect Helmut Jahn. This almost understated building is subtly instrumental in a revitalization of the IIT campus and realization of Mies van der Rohe's urban landscape master plan, developed in 1939 and redeveloped in 1995 by Mies' grandson Dirk Lohan.

Two important buildings have been carried out at the center of the recent plan. The McCormick Tribune Campus Center designed by Rem Koolhaas with OMA (Office for Metropolitan Architecture) is built around the existing commons building by Mies from 1953, gathering student activity at the center of campus. Also, the State Street Village student dormitory offers university apartment living with a corporate character. Conveniently located adjacent to campus center, it is a sort of Miesian agora with modern amenities, creating a protected atmospheric interior world sheltered from the neighboring "El" elevated train line.

This stylish dormitory not only helps connect the campus buildings around as a backdrop, it acts as a shield from the existing train line as well as a dazzling art piece. A new era is introduced with limitless fantasy; a symbiosis of architecture and landscape lies at the heart and energy of the project. Light floods the rooms of this brilliant plan and represents the continuing revolution of an ever-developing transparent architecture that is not only economical but offers a legendary address for its inhabitants. One sees the fundamental roots of design in its construction and play of light. A simple elegance comes through with its complexity and openness. In this project Helmut Jahn has brought forth his statement with attention to its setting and integration into the campus posed between active, partially enclosed courtyards planted with birch trees that bring the campus life into, and at some points through, the building. A promenade through the structure encourages its daily use and creates an almost transparent transition from the outside into the inside. One's sense

CROWN HALL, IIT, LUDWIG MIES VAN DER ROHE
DRAWING/COLLAGE ©2000 PAO-CHI CHANG

of perception is altered by the use of form. From this creative dialogue between inside and outside comes an exemplary design that purifies and is the architectural embodiment of the current public awareness with traditions taken from Mies and his campus plan, demonstrating advances in architecture and technology without a loss of quality. This is State Street Village.

In today's construction world there is a transitional relationship from subjective concepts to realized objective requirements. The embodiment of form and shape with technology is clearly implemented. The creative challenge for the architect is to mesh the technical and the aesthetic. To achieve this balance Helmut Jahn has collaborated with many other disciplines. He worked closely with engineer Werner Sobek to explore potential structural solutions and coordinated with environmental consultant Mathias Schuler. Thus, a collaboration was formed to tap the full potential of building technology with the commitment to accomplish it. From

this team, sustainable energy usage and efficient building structure have been achieved. The underlying principle to improve and integrate technology with architecture was a guiding tenet and is evident in this technologically advanced, efficient and strong-minded structure, showing an enthusiasm that challenges the times and pushes the thought process.

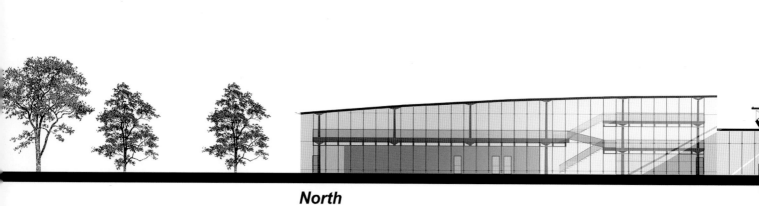

North

West

S-33

HELMUT JAHN ENTRY FOR STUDENT UNION COMPETITION, 1998

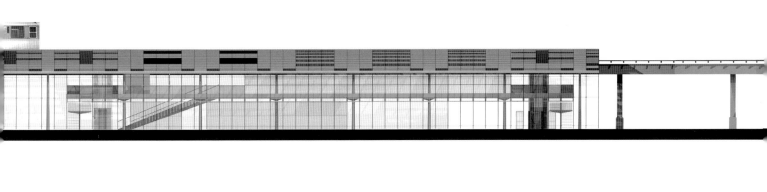

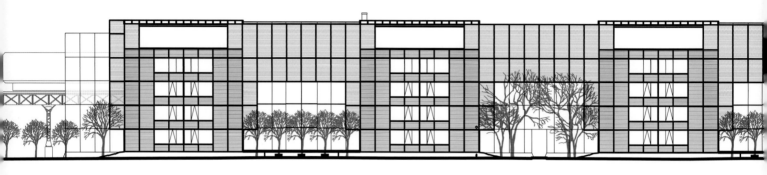

West Elevation

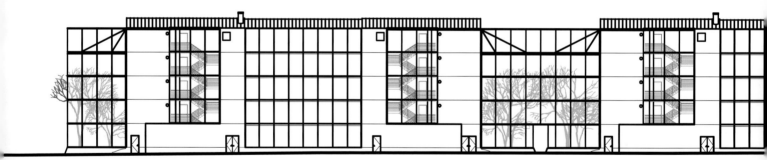

East Elevation

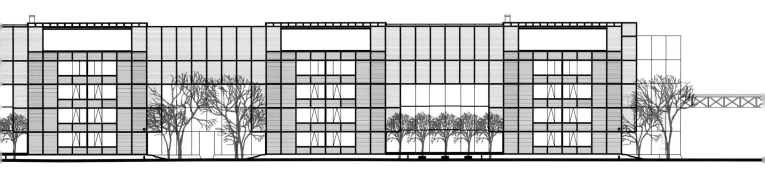

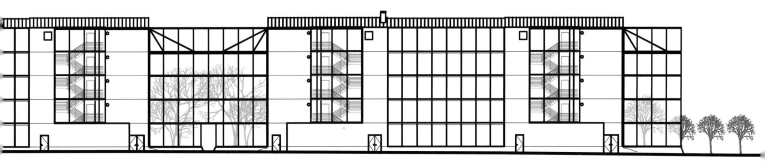

0   20   40   60 ft.

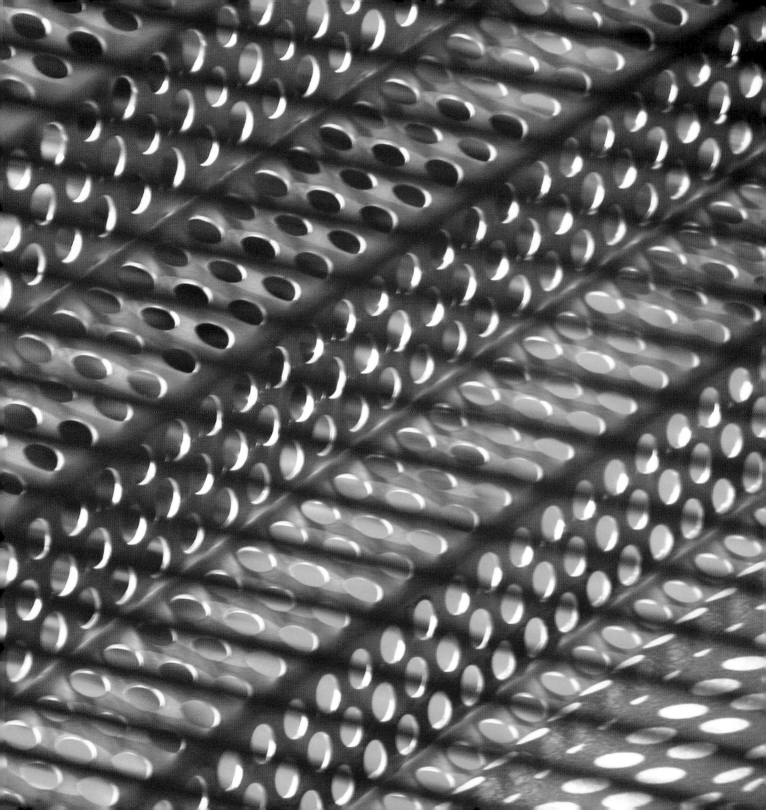

STATE STREET VILLAGE DESCRIPTION

HELMUT JAHN

Through an invited competition we won the commission for the IIT Student Housing.

The site, across the college's main quadrangle and Mies' Crown Hall, had to respond both to the quadrangle as a space-defining wall, as well be pervious, allowing east-west movement through the campus, which is divided through the north-south barriers of State Street and the elevated train.

Between three U-shaped buildings forming entry courts are two sallyports. Towards the elevated train, glass screens protect from their noise. The curved west façade of profiled stainless steel panels transitions at the set-back-floor into the roof and reinforces the idea of an extrusion. At the courts and sallyports the wall projects and the panels are perforated and form screened gates.

The low budget did not allow planning for long-term energy/comfort measures in the MEP system. However, the comfort of the user has been improved by simple means, like coated, low-E glass, maximizing daylight and natural ventilation, and a specially designed furniture system allowing the students maximum flexibility in placement and use.

The earlier unbuilt project for the Campus Center occupied partially the same site. Its program and use led to a building of components, which are flexible, adaptable and exchangeable over the buildings' life. The housing project did not require such a strategy, but resulted in a clear response to the urban condition with a bold curved form and industrial materials facing the rigor of the Mies-Campus.

STATE STREET VILLAGE OPENING

HELMUT JAHN, JULY 22, 2003

This opening is connected to a long time span in my personal and professional life and therefore, I cannot avoid connecting this history with today's event.

In September 2003 it will be 37 years ago when I settled into a dorm at IIT, right behind the new building.

I enrolled in Graduate School and was told not to leave the campus or go to the lake (I did anyway.) I had to cross State Street and the El to get to my dorm.

I started working part-time for Gene Summers and even in the big snow storm of 1967 I fought my way to the El and to his office on Ontario Street.

I loved the El and this building shows it. It does not hide the El, it rather integrates and celebrates it, yet the building reduces its noise.

Much of what I know and made me a "real" architect I learned in those two years at school. Mies was not teaching anymore, but Hilbersheimer, Brenner and Danforth were there and most rewarding were the Saturday sessions with Myron Goldsmith and Faz Khan.

The campus had seen the building of the new library and Hermann Hall by Walter Netsch of SOM. Subsequently, Myron Goldsmith did the new gym and other academic buildings, adapting the Miesian idiom by incorporating new available principles of engineering and technology.

When I got involved in rebuilding McCormick Place with Gene Summers and C.F. Murphy in 1967, my class attendance dropped and in 1968 I went on a leave of absence, which I am still on.

After a longer pause it was the deanships of Gene Summers and Dona Robertson, which brought me and other Murphy/Jahn personnel to the school.

The Pritzker/Galvin grant enabled IIT to take the necessary steps into the future by renewing its academic program and starting an ambitious building program for new structures and restoring the "Mies" Campus.

Based on a Master Plan by Dirk Lohan the new Campus Center and SSV are the first buildings in what was before a divisive nowhere land between the residential campus in the east and the academic campus in the west.

State Street Village treats the east edge of the campus quadrangle as a space-defining wall, which at the same time allows east-west movement through the campus and informing future development east of the El. Those two "sallyports" are in between three u-shaped buildings with more private entry courts. Roof terraces overlook the quadrangle, the campus and the city skyline. Perforated screens span the courts and Sallyports and tie the buildings together into a long, curved extrusion. Towards the El, glass screens cut the noise while keeping the trains visible and adding an aspect of mobility, which provides a special experience of speed and freedom. The building alludes to the streamlined trains and objects of the Art Moderne of the 20s. It is a simple and clear diagram translated into a three-dimensional object.

Above the pragmatic task of attending to the urban, functional, technical, cost and time issues the intellectual task at hand was "What to do after Mies?" In a time with no concurrence on style, the "anything goes" possibilities of digital imaging this building stands for an attitude that progress and new expression in architecture comes not so much from form and style, but through integrating architecture, engineering and a straightforward expression of its components, materials and parts in their construction. Energy and comfort measures have been addressed by simple means within the low budget: maximizing daylight, coated glass, natural ventilation, an interactive way to reduce the El noise and a specially designed furniture system allowing the students maximum flexibility in placement and use.

I hope we have provided IIT with a product that exceeds their goals. It is not only the 370 beds which needed to be accommodated, but to give the residents an added living experience and more comfort, the University a more vital and attractive infrastructure and to set standards of quality which enthuse students, faculty, the university, alumni and the city with the promise of IIT's future.

OVERVIEW
LYNN BECKER

How do you build after Mies? How do you confront Mies on the seminal campus that he designed, in a city whose landmarks offer up a 125-year timeline of modern architecture's evolution? Those were the questions that Helmut Jahn faced, and he describes State Street Village as his "intellectual answer."

To understand that answer, you have to look back, before even Mies, to Louis Sullivan, and his championing of an "organic" architecture. "Form follows function" is the inspiration he took from the way form in plants was an expression of their function. "The oak tree expressed the function oak, the pine tree expressed the function pine," he said in way of example. Never the clearest of writers, Sullivan's explanation is little more than a tautology, but in his great buildings the idea can be seen with absolute clarity. The elevations frankly express their structural steel frame. The lightness and openness of those frames, along with the increasing use of glass, marked the beginning point of liberating architecture from the aesthetic and structural constraints of the load-bearing wall, putting it on a path that led to the transparency of today's design.

Sullivan's large windows with moveable sashes brought natural light and air deep into the interiors, but that was as much a matter of economic necessity as design. His preferred way of bringing nature to his works was as a mimetic applied finish, an amazingly intricate foliate ornament, expressed in stencil, cast-iron and terra cotta, that flows over the surfaces of his buildings like a fecund wash.

By the time Mies arrived in Chicago in 1938, Sullivan's message had been largely forgotten. Structure was still entombed in heavy, non-load bearing masonry. Mies's genius was to understand how emerging technology could empower his own search for essence, for an architecture of "almost nothing." The ancient carapace was cracked and discarded, the light skeleton revealed. Glass was no longer a puncture in a solid wall, but the wall itself. Transparency was now the link to nature, bringing the outside into the building. In the Chicago Loop of 1955, that outside world was often a hard backdrop of stone and brick, thickly begrimed with decades of coal dust, but at Mies van der Rohe's Crown Hall, it was an IIT campus where his elegantly simple buildings sat within a spacious landscape of trees, lawns, fountains, flowers and birds. Crown Hall looked forward to a new world of cleaner burning fuels and a renewed attention to the quality of the urban environment. The organic was no longer expressed in applied ornament, but in an opening up to nature.

At Crown Hall, there's also still natural ventilation through a continuous ring of operable vents, but just as architecture steamrolled past Sullivan's idea of an organic architecture over a half-century before, Mies's early experiments with natural air and light were soon forgotten in the era's access to cheap energy. As floor plates swelled in size and air conditioning became ubiquitous, the norm for a modern building soon became a sealed glass box with artificial ventilation, often running in overdrive to compensate for the heat funneled into the interior by the solar gain. At IIT, Mies's own designs became riddled with punctures for vents and duct work.

Today, as energy costs explode and environmental awareness swells, new technologies are creating a range of possibilities for incorporating natural processes into architecture that Sullivan or Mies could never have imagined. The "organic" no longer means applying emulations of leaves and flowers to a façade to remind us of nature. In State Street Village, Helmut Jahn, along with Murphy/Jahn's John Durbrow, has created a building where "organic" refers not to applied ornament, but to its handling of light, air, sound and circulation, and to the way the varied textures of its materials form an expressive fabric of visual grace and balance.

State Street Village engages, rather than rebuffs, the urban environment, putting it in sharp contrast to more traditional designs, such as Ricardo Legoretta's new Max Palevsky Residential Commons at the University of Chicago. Set within an older neo-gothic campus, the Palevsky Commons consists of three buildings separated by a driveway and walkthrough that provide pedestrian access to the courtyards stashed behind the complex. The front elevations along 56th Street congeal into an 800-foot-long Chinese wall of heavy brick and punched windows with thick concrete surrounds, relieved only by a glass curtain wall marking the center building's entrance lobby and by semi-detached steel and glass pavilions at the outer buildings' corners. The essence of modern architec-

ture — its lightness and transparency — is segregated on the periphery, to keep it from competing with the sentimental visual qualities of traditional masonry.

Architecture is a dialectic between past and future. The U of C dorms, reflecting their gothic surroundings and the idea of university as refuge, evoke a traditional bulwark to a filthy-aired, anarchic city that no longer exists. State Street Village, set within the open, modernist tableau of the Mies IIT campus, looks forward. Jahn is quick to dismiss facile analogies between transparency and democracy, yet it's hard not to conclude that the openness of today's architecture marks a liberation from the pandemic anxiety over the external world that created the fortress-like buildings of past eras. Like the best work of Mies, SSV is prototypically an expression of our time, not in postmodernist sense of the latest fashion, but in how advances in technology are used to address student preferences for a mode of living that updates the traditional dorm to incorporate more of the experience of contemporary urban condominiums and apartments.

The hallmark of State Street Village's architecture is its permeability. The five courtyards all face the street and provide pathways that cut through the complex. Along the shorter ends of the building, and enclosing the courtyards, glass curtain walls bring light into the dorms. Operable windows give residents access to natural ventilation. Along State Street itself, the facing consists entirely of perforated stainless steel panels in just two varieties — solid or perforated — yet the alteration of those two contrasting qualities creates a texture whose richly varied rhythm, along with the broad strips of windows, expels any sense of heaviness from the long façade.

Light is as integral an element in this building as the physical materials of concrete, steel and glass. It dematerializes the structure's bulk and, like a chameleon whose camouflage is not color but porosity, transforms its appearance throughout the day according to the presence and position of the sun. At night, the screens across the front of the courtyards that appeared almost solid in late afternoon are backlit into translucence. In the morning, they'll look nearly transparent as the sun rises in the sky. (On the other side of the screens — within the courtyards themselves — the process runs in reverse.)

In Louis Sullivan's day, before air conditioning and just beyond the gas lamp, providing maximum light and air was a simple economic necessity, and the organic a matter of pasting over a building with reminders of nature. Mies's transparency opened buildings up to the world around them, but by the time of this death, they had become slaves to mechanical systems that were increasingly demanding and expensive. In our own time, technology offers the possibility of creating buildings that breathe and cool and warm and protect in a way that reflects the processes of our own bodies. At State Street Village the perforations in the stainless steel panels transmit light and air much like pores aspirate our skin. "Form follows function" begins to take on a new and deeper meaning.

DORMITORY RESIDENT

AMANDA JANE BOTWAY
ARCHITECTURE STUDENT, SOPHOMORE

One never expects to go off to college and live in the most desirable dormitory in the country, but it happened to me. As an architecture student at the Illinois Institute of Technology in Chicago, I have discovered that great architecture is all around me in Chicago. However, it wasn't until I saw it through the breathtaking views at State Street Village that I could truly appreciate it.

Designed by world-renowned architect, Helmut Jahn, State Street Village is by far the greatest advancement in college living since the creation of dormitories. The amenities include: suite style dorms with private bathrooms, individually controlled climates, wall to wall soundproof glass windows, full kitchens, laundry facilities, common areas on each floor, a lounge with 42" plasma flat screen televisions and surround sound, custom designed furniture, fifth floor balconies offering panoramic views of Chicago, landscaped courtyards, glass elevators and 24-hour security with keyless entry to residents. Our newest amenity is the ability and convenience to check the status of our laundry online.

The five-story complex, comprised of one third apartments and two thirds suite-style dormitories, is also a convenient place to live. It is located in the heart of campus with the new student center across the street. There is also plenty of parking behind the building. Chicago's famous El train is just steps away and takes you directly downtown in a matter of minutes.

State Street Village offers a bird's eye view of city life. The building has huge windows with a perfect view of the campus, the city and of course the Green Line El trains. When you step off the glass elevator and walk in to the commons you are often greeted by the train passing by. It is like watching a movie with the mute button on. You can hardly hear it through the soundproof glass.

The building is designed to look like a streamline train. It fits perfectly into the surroundings. There is also a spectacular view of the sunrise reflected off the back of the building: the whole thing glows! After living in the dormitory for a year, I can honestly say I love it. It has everything a college student could ever dream of and more. My favorite parts of all are seeing the fireworks from a White Sox game go off and watching downtown light up as the sun goes down. State Street Village truly is a wonderful place to live.

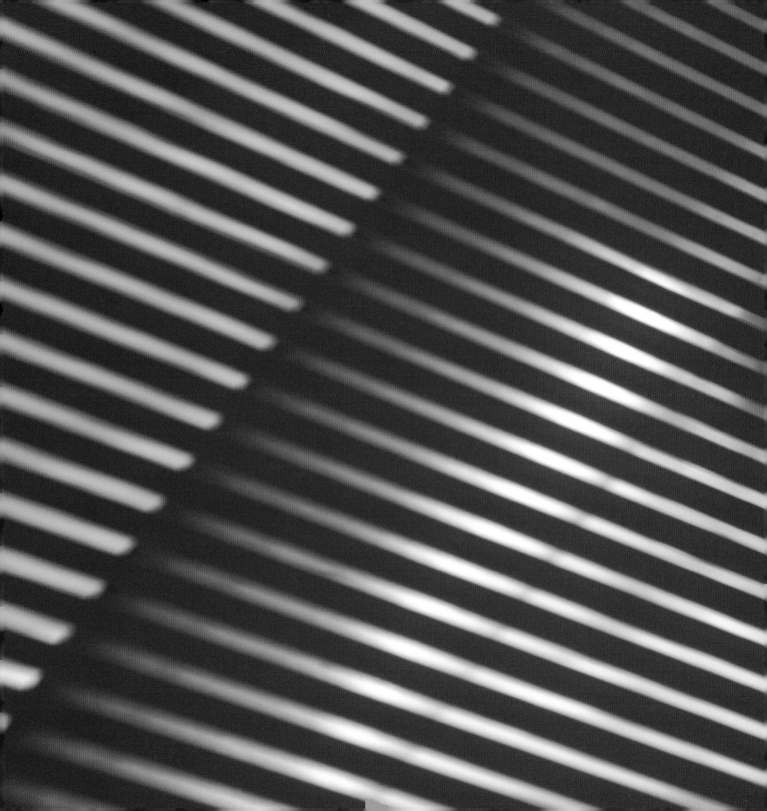

BUILDING

LYNN BECKER

State Street Village offered its architects a number of challenges. It had to address the noise of the El. It had to help re-unify the campus. The budget was an austere $18,700,000. And it had to be built quickly. Some of the more environmentally advanced systems designed by Jahn collaborator Matthias Schuler had to be cut. IIT maintains its own steam plant, and State Street Village had originally anticipated adding a source of chilled water and using radiant coils in the ceiling slabs to heat and cool the dorms. In the end, SSV wound up with forced air. Originally proposed to be constructed out of precast cored planks, the structure would end up being poured-in-place concrete.

In layout, State Street Village is a standard box, the columns placed on 20-foot centers north/south and 14-foot east/west, in parallel to the actual dimensions of the dorm rooms. There are no funky-shaped spaces — round, pie-shaped or otherwise — just the traditional rectangles. Extrapolate that layout to SSV's full 525-foot length, and you have a recipe for overbearing monotony. Yet what looks to be one structure is actually six pavilions paired into three buildings, interspersed by five courtyards, "a kind of punctuated extrusion," says Jahn. A single bold gesture purges the design of any sense of the traditional glass box. Along State Street, the façade and roofline appear as a single, gracefully curving plane, flaring out at its base, its surfaces alternating between solid and permeable.

Within that plane, windows are set flush within a surface of corrugated stainless steel. At the edges of each pavilion, and at the ends of the building itself, the ribs are perforated, forming screens that provide privacy while allowing the free flow of light and air. At the fourth floor, the plane curves backward, and the stainless steel panels form bands that extend without interruption across the full length of the building, uniting its six pavilions into a single form.

At the top, the fifth floor, the floorplate steps back to half the depth of the floors below, accommodating a series of student lounges, each fronted by an outdoor terrace that's left open to the sky. Next to them, the screen over each courtyard continues curving backward to meet the corners of the front wall of the lounges, the perforated ribs often casting a rich texture of shadows along the arching steel members that support them. At the ends of the building, the screens stretch all the way back to the rear façade, the end segment forming an overhanging cornice, completing the curving sweep that hovers over the building's mass like a graceful benediction.

The Spartan eastern elevation of State Street Village has a definite back-alley feel, yet its perpendiculars of bare concrete, framing the glass expanses of the courtyards and exposed stairways, mirrors the raw industrial feel of the El tracks, which runs past it at mid-height like a horizontal coursing. Approaching the building from the east is like a cleansing of the visual palette, a spare simplicity before encountering the varied landscaping and rich structural textures that lie beyond the sallyport.

"We were told that they liked our building," says Jahn, "but they didn't think we could build it for the budget. We went through several months of refining and I think everybody believed this was doable. The swing element — which was not originally contracted for — was actually all the windwalls, the screen walls, and the sound walls. You could save a million dollars not putting those things in, but in the end, they were really essential to the physical and visual success and working of the building. With all the rooms facing into the courtyards, not towards the El, we were able to reduce the sound and use natural ventilation."

Jahn is now extending what he learned at State Street Village to an innovative SRO (Single Room Occupancy) project on the city's near north side. He's optimistic

he'll be able to incorporate some of the advanced technology that got trimmed at SSV: solar panels, wind turbines, collecting rainwater for irrigation, gray water to flush the toilets. Elsewhere in the city, we're still waiting for developers to catch on. In Chicago, the courtyard building basically stopped evolving in the 1920s. It's a sedate, vaguely Prairie School styled brick structure around a central courtyard usually landscaped in scruffy, untended vegetation. In State Street Village, Helmut Jahn not only creates a new model for student housing, but also points a possible alternative to the gracelessly monolithic, cinder-block condos that are overtaking so many of the city's neighborhoods.

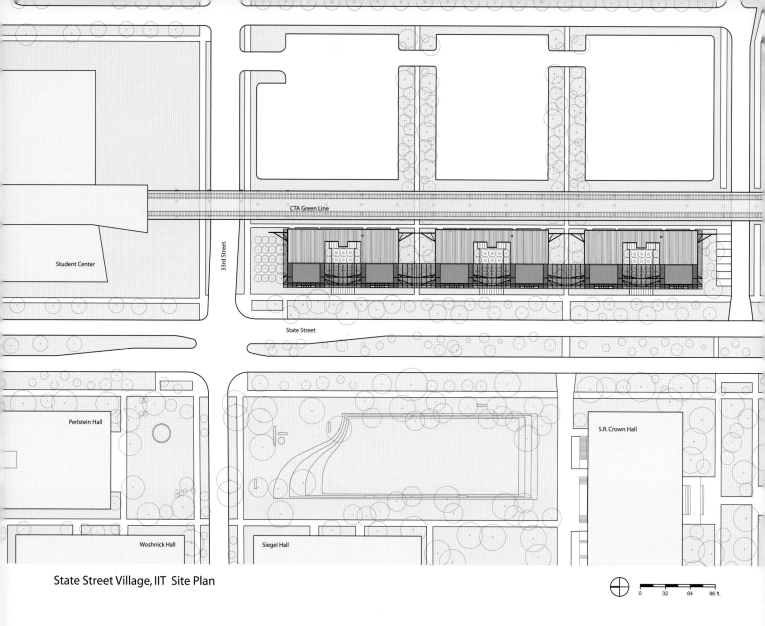

State Street Village, IIT Site Plan

CTA Green Line

33rd Street

State Street

Student Center

Perlstein Hall

S.R. Crown Hall

Woshnick Hall

Siegel Hall

0   32   64   96 ft.

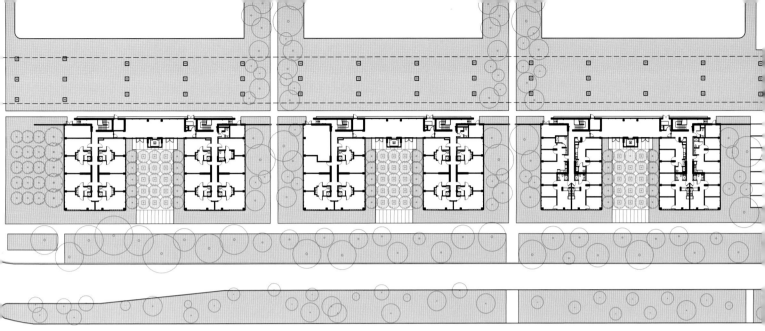

Ground Floor Plan

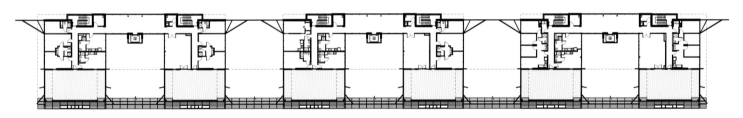

Fifth Floor Plan

State Street Village, IIT Overview Plan

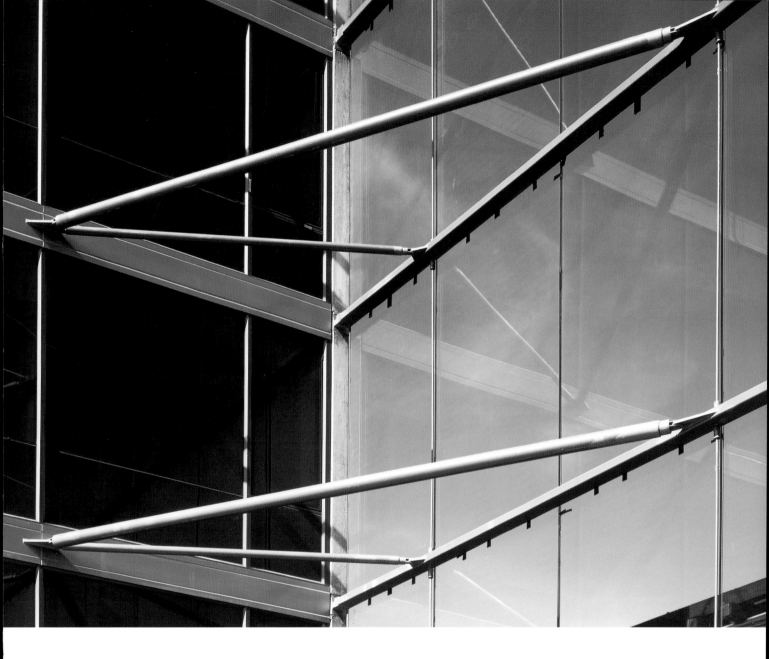

COURTYARDS AND SALLYPORTS

LYNN BECKER

The courtyards and sallyports of State Street Village are the elements that both let the building breathe and stitch it into the urban context of the surrounding IIT campus. Generously landscaped, they provide a softening intercession of nature into the harder machine-fabricated presence of the structure.

They are also the building's incubators of light, bringing it into the individual dorms and using it to animate the perforated stainless steel screens that rise up over each courtyard like a proscenium, drawing, says Jahn, on "the idea of the scrim. Those spaces become like a stage set viewed from the street or across the street. It's like on a stage, if the light is behind the scrim, the scrim is transparent. If the light is in front the scrim, it becomes solid. So there is this ever-changing appearance." The screens also help make the courtyards a summer refuge. The solid portion of the panels diffuses the glare of the hot sun, while the perforations let cooling breezes flow freely.

Open to the street at the front, the courtyards are enclosed with glass curtain walls on the other three sides.

Along the back, the twinned pavilions of each of the three buildings are connected by a glass-enclosed "bridge" structure, housing the entry-level lobby and upper-story lounges, all opening off an elevator encased in its own slim, glass tower. In the other two courtyards that separate the three buildings, sallyports pierce the rear glass "sound walls," providing a connection that allows students to move freely between the residential campus to the east and the academic campus to the west. The sound walls, which also extend a full twenty-four feet beyond each end of SSV, shield the building from the noise of the El. Suspended from the building with long-armed tubular steel brackets, and set in a threadlike structure of thin aluminum spandrels, the sound walls seem almost to float, so light in appearance that they look like they'd crumple in the first heavy gust, but, in fact, painstakingly engineered to withstand any load the windy city can muster.

Along the sides, the curtain walls that stream light into the dorms are a delicate balancing of strong linear spandrels and super-thin mullions. The glass has a reflective gray tint that both reduces solar gain and offers a warm counterpoint to the cool steel of the façade.

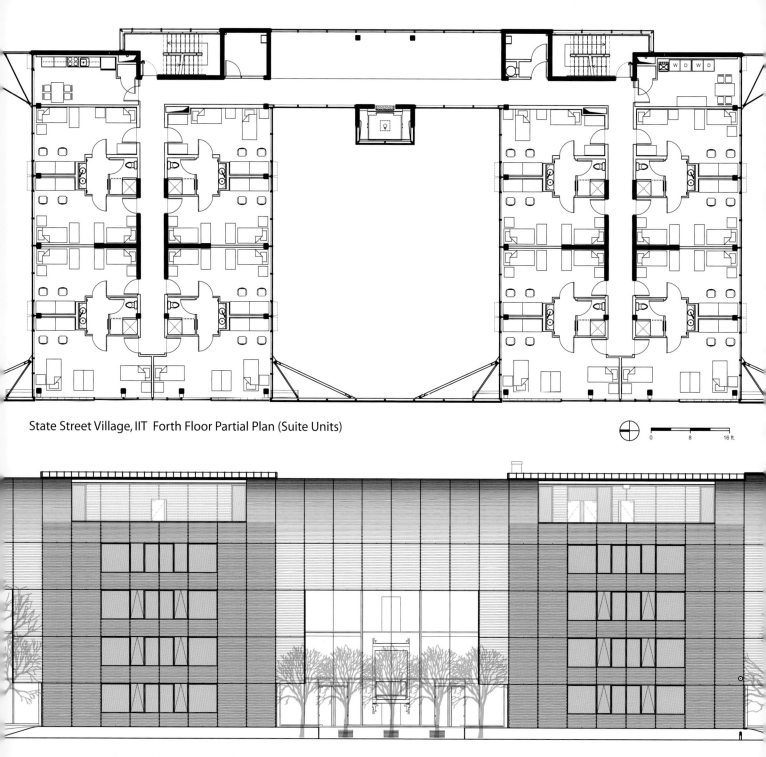

State Street Village, IIT Forth Floor Partial Plan (Suite Units)

0   8   16 ft.

State Street Village, IIT Partial West Elevation

0   8   16 ft.

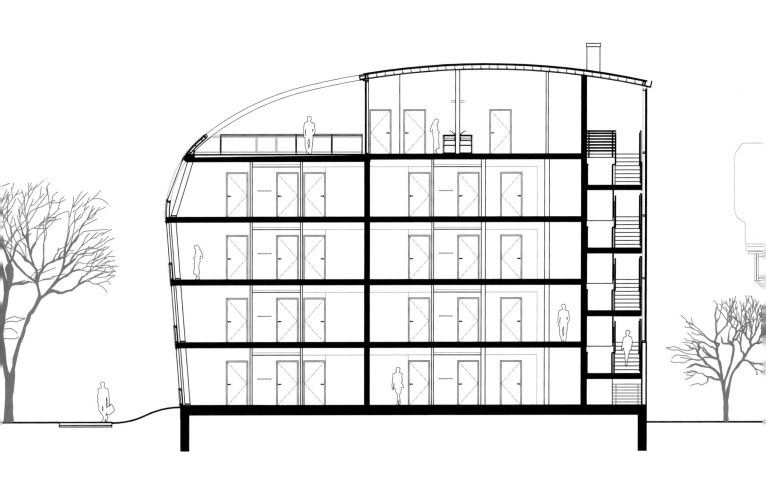

State Street Village, IIT Transverse Section

0   4   8   12 ft.

HABITAT
LYNN BECKER

The approaches that Jahn and Rem Koolhaas, who designed the new Student Center to the north of SSV, employ in dealing with the problem of the El illustrate contrasting responses to the urban condition. Koolhaas's is reminiscent of the way Frank Lloyd Wright, in a building such as Robie House, creates a slightly fortress-like refuge that turns its back on the street. To muffle the noise of the El, Koolhaas pushes it off into the 530-foot-long tube that has quickly become a symbol of the campus. Jahn, who as an IIT student was a regular user of public transit — his own dorm was kitty-korner from the site of State Street Village — makes the El a part of the design. Sitting in one of the glass-walled elevator lounges, it looks like you could almost reach out and touch the trains as they rush past, only meters away, their roar tamed by the dual-paned glass to an almost subliminal rumble. Putting the lounges and stairways at the back of the building also provides an additional buffer between the dorms and the El.

There are more student lounges on the top floor, complete with wide-screen flat-panel televisions. Just outside, in another example of the way State Street Village engages and embraces the urban environment, broad rooftop terraces provide spectacular views of the IIT campus to the west and the Chicago skyline to the north.

Walls, floors and ceilings are most often bare concrete, far from the often riotous colors of Jahn's early, postmodernist buildings like the Thompson Center and Citicorp Center/Ogilvie Station. The students them-selves provide the color: in the elevator lounges, the postings taped to the gray concrete are on a rainbow of different hues of paper.

The same simplicity carries through to the dorms them-selves — exposed concrete posts, ceilings and walls, white drywall along the interior of the façade, simple epoxy floors, and furniture, also designed by Murphy/Jahn, in stainless steel frames with black wood infills. It's not surprising that in the model dorms, towels, bedspreads and accessories are all in bright primary colors.

Wireless connectivity is provided throughout the building, and students can even check out the status of laundry room washers and dryers on the internet, but the true luxury of the dorms lies in their generous measure of space, light and air. On average, they're about twice the size of the dorm rooms Mies built in the 1950s. Bathrooms are no longer down the hall, but open up directly off the dorm rooms. Where dorm rooms are paired, with a bathroom between them, each room still has its own entrance. Apartment-style dorms in the southernmost building even include their own kitchens.

Each dorm offers a generous expanse of windows, many of which open to allow for natural ventilation. The glass is designed to be more tinted than transparent, and along the courtyards and end walls the bottom light is fritted, providing an additional measure of privacy.

Dorms along State Street have an added bonus. The outer wall flares subtly outward along the plane of the angled façade, as do the windows, and the ceiling slabs

become thinner as they meet the façade, flooding the room with light and providing an added sense of spaciousness. For an architecture student, these are million-dollar rooms. For no extra charge, you get to wake up each morning, inspired — and perhaps a bit intimidated — by the sight of Mies van der Rohe's Crown Hall, one of the icons of modern architecture, just outside your window.

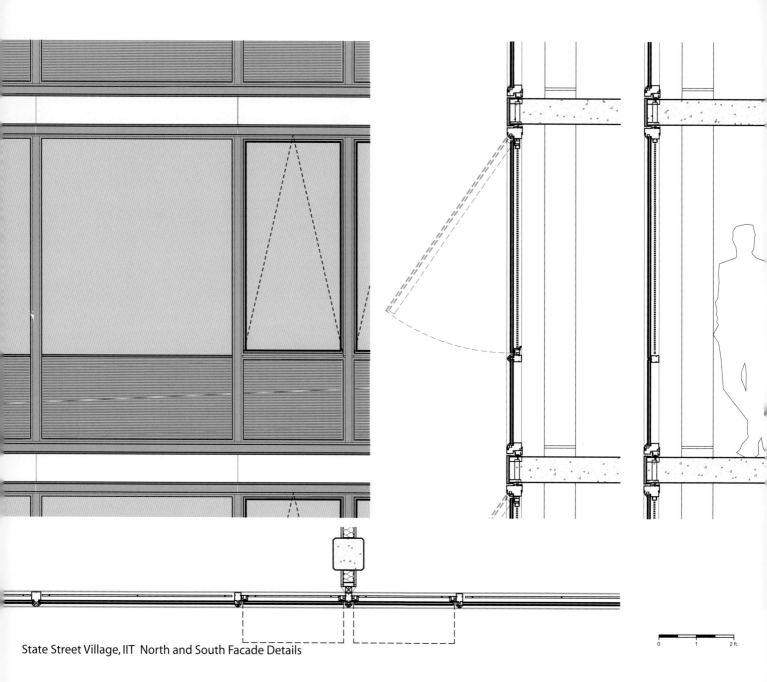

State Street Village, IIT North and South Facade Details

0   1   2 ft.

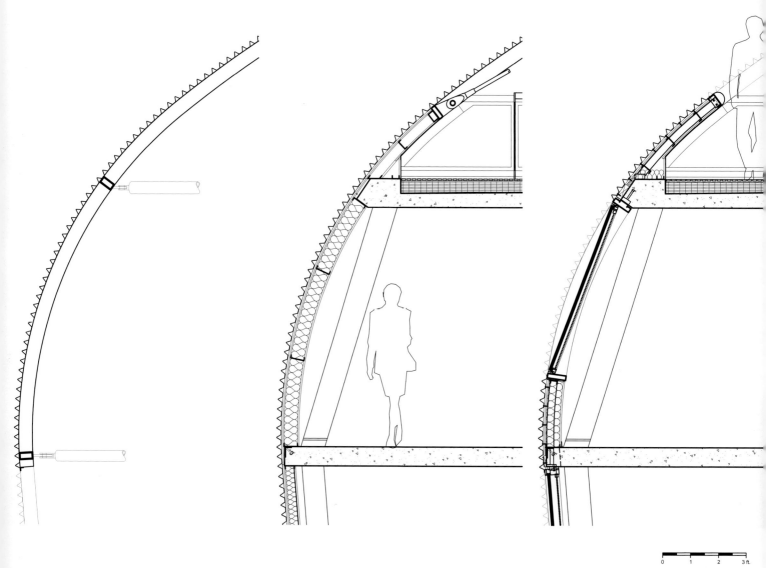

State Street Village, IIT Facade Details

ACKNOWLEDGMENTS

Illinois Institute of Technology: Lew Collens, John Collins, Tom Meyer, Dona Robertson.

Murphy/Jahn: Helmut Jahn, John Durbrow, Sam Scaccia, Peter Hayes, Chad Mitchell, Dan Cubric, Francisco Gonzalez-Pulido, Naotami Yasuda, Salim Bou-Saab, John Manaves.

Structural Engineers: WSI – Werner Sobek.

Energy/Comfort: Transsolar – Matthias Schuler.

Landscape: Peter Schaudt.

Furniture: Michael Heltzer.

Contractor: W. O'Neill – Oleh Karawan, Executive Vice President; Hans Thilenius, Senior Project Manager.

Sub Contractors: Mero Structures – Sound/Screen Walls, Arcadia – Glass Facade.